D1325889

EXTREME

Storm Chaser

Dicing With the World's Most Deadly Storms

Clive Gifford

A & C Black • London

Produced for A & C Black by
 Monkey Puzzle Media Ltd
Little Manor Farm, Brundish,
Woodbridge, Suffolk IP13 8BL, UK

Published by A & C Black Publishers Limited
36 Soho Square, London W1D 3QY

First published 2009

Editor: Susie Brooks
Design: Mayer Media Ltd
Picture research: Lynda Lines
Series consultants: Jane Turner and James de Winter

This book is produced using paper that is made
from wood grown in managed, sustainable forests.
It is natural, renewable and recyclable. The logging
and manufacturing processes conform to the
environmental regulations of the country of origin.

Printed in Singapore by Tien Wah Press (Pte.) Ltd

Picture acknowledgements
Alamy pp. 1 (A T Willett), 9 (A T Willett), 18–19
(Ryan McGinnis), 24–25 (Ryan McGinnis); Corbis
pp. 4–5 (Reuters), 6–7 (Johnathan Smith/Cordaiy
Photo Library Ltd), 12 (Shannon Stapleton), 22 (Phil
Klein), 24 (Tom Bean), 28–29 (Danny Gawlowski/
Dallas Morning News), 29 right (Larry Smith/epa);
Getty Images pp. 4 left (Jim Reed), 8, 10 (AFP),
12–13, 14, 16 (Jim Reed), 18 (Jim Reed), 20 (Carsten
Peter), 26–27, 27 right (Science Faction); Photoshot
p. 21 (Marlin Levison); Rex Features pp. 6, 26 left
(Sipa Press); Science Photo Library pp. 11
(Planetobserver), 16–17 (Jim Reed), 22–23 (Kent
Wood); Topfoto.co.uk p. 14–15 (ImageWorks).

The front cover shows tornadoes on the horizon
(Getty Images/Peter Rauter).

Every effort has been made to contact copyright
holders of material reproduced in this book. Any
omissions will be rectified in subsequent printings if
notice is given to the publishers.

CONTENTS

Abbreviations **km** stands for kilometres • **m** stands for metres • **ft** stands for feet • **cm** stands for centimetres • **in** stands for inches • **km/h** stands for kilometres per hour • **mph** stands for miles per hour • **kg** stands for kilograms

Smashing time

Imagine storm clouds the size of mountains coming to smash up your city. The chances are you'd run for your life – unless you were a storm chaser.

When the weather gets mean, storm chasers race to the scene. They are always hunting for storms to study, photograph and film. Some do it just for the thrill. Others are serious scientists who report back to weather services. All are amazed, and sometimes terrified, by the power of the storms they find.

*Storm chaser Mike Theiss films the **storm surge** during Hurricane Katrina in New Orleans, USA, in 2005.*

Fastest ever

Storm-chasing scientist Dr Josh Wurman measured a **tornado** that struck Oklahoma City, USA, in 1999. Its wind speeds reached 509 kilometres per hour (316 miles per hour) – the fastest ever recorded on Earth.

Part of Oklahoma City lies in ruins after a series of tornadoes in 1999.

storm surge a swell of water pushed to the shore by storm winds

Emergency vehicles arrive at the scene.

The mighty winds ripped buildings to the ground.

Cars were thrown off the road.

tornado a spinning, funnel-shaped windstorm

5

Trouble brewing

Sometimes fluffy white clouds aren't as harmless as they look. High above in the Earth's atmosphere, they could be brewing something scary...

Storms happen when warm air meets cold air in the atmosphere. Warm, moist air rises upwards, sometimes in a powerful stream called an **updraft**. As it travels higher and meets colder air, it cools, and millions of tiny water droplets form. These are what we see as clouds.

Storm clouds can produce driving winds and rain.

atmosphere the layer of gases that surround the Earth

Thunderheads

Towering cumulonimbus clouds are a tell-tale sign that a storm is coming.

Huge storm clouds often spread out at their top as high winds in the atmosphere blow them around. The result is called an anvil top.

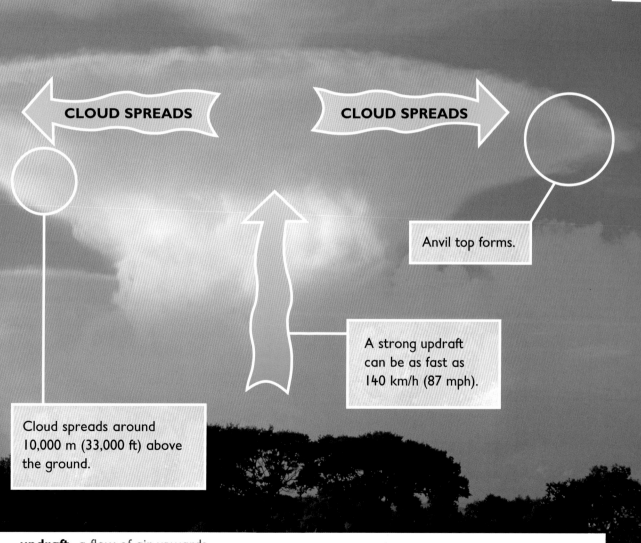

CLOUD SPREADS

CLOUD SPREADS

Anvil top forms.

A strong updraft can be as fast as 140 km/h (87 mph).

Cloud spreads around 10,000 m (33,000 ft) above the ground.

updraft a flow of air upwards

In a twister

Tornadoes, nicknamed twisters, are enough to make you dizzy – or even dead. These fast-spinning storms act like vicious vacuum cleaners, sucking up and smashing everything in their path.

This woman's house stood no chance against a tornado, with winds lashing at over 280 km/h (174 mph).

Shredder!

All the rocks, wood and other objects sucked up by a tornado whirl around. Like massive spinning blades, they scrape, slash and shatter anything they hit.

Tornadoes begin in thunderclouds and then swirl downwards, twisting and turning. Their power is terrifying. As they spin, air is forced away from the middle of the tornado. This creates a **vacuum** that can suck up cars and buildings and rip trees out of the ground.

vacuum a completely empty, airless space

Most tornadoes are less than 200 m (656 ft) across.

Wind races round and up in the **vortex**.

Wind speed = up to 500 km/h (310 mph)

Tornado turns a dirty brown because of all the bits and pieces it picks up.

The storm must reach the ground before it can be called a tornado.

A giant twister moves through green wheat fields in Texas, USA.

The edge of the tornado funnel can twist, bend and rip apart buildings.

vortex a whirling mass of air that sucks in everything near it

Tornado Alley

Houses flattened by a tornado in Oklahoma. Oklahoma suffers more tornadoes than any other US state.

Could you get caught in a tornado? They happen in Australia, Asia, Africa and parts of Europe. But there's one place that gets the twister treatment more than anywhere else. Welcome to Tornado Alley, USA!

In the central USA, the land is mainly flat. Cold, dry air from Canada flows across it one way while warm, wet air from the Gulf of Mexico heads in from the opposite direction. Twisters strike when these two streams of air collide – mostly in Tornado Alley. No wonder it's a storm chaser's favourite place.

Still centre

In 1951, Roy Hall saw inside a tornado when it ripped the roof off his house. He was thrown about, but survived to see the centre of the tornado pass over. Another tornado survivor, Will Keller, said the centre was, "as still as death".

2008: A tornado flattens half the city of Parkersburg, Iowa.

Tornado Alley is shaded in yellow on this map. Over 500 twisters strike here every year — we've labelled some of the big ones.

COLD, DRY AIR

CANADA

1999: A deadly tornado **swarm** strikes Oklahoma City.

USA

TORNADO ALLEY

1979: At Wichita Falls, Texas, a tornado injures 1,700 people.

1999: Tornadoes destroy the town of Jarrell, Texas.

WARM, DAMP AIR

MEXICO

GULF OF MEXICO

swarm a series of tornadoes produced by the same storm

Hurry, it's a hurricane!

A hurricane is like a tornado's big brother. It may creep up slowly – but be warned. There are devastating amounts of energy in their whirling winds.

A storm becomes a hurricane once its wind speeds are at least 119 kilometres per hour (74 miles per hour). Hurricanes form over warm ocean waters, where rising heat helps them to grow in size and power. The biggest hurricanes can measure hundreds of kilometres across. If they reach land, trouble is guaranteed.

A fireman wades through floods left by Hurricane Katrina in New Orleans, USA. The storm caused more than 1,800 deaths and over US$80 billion of damage.

satellite   a machine that is sent into space to collect and send back information

Nice name!

Every hurricane has its own name!
The list goes in alphabetical order
and from girl to boy to girl...

A **satellite** photograph captures Hurricane
Katrina on 29 August 2005, the day it
began destroying New Orleans.

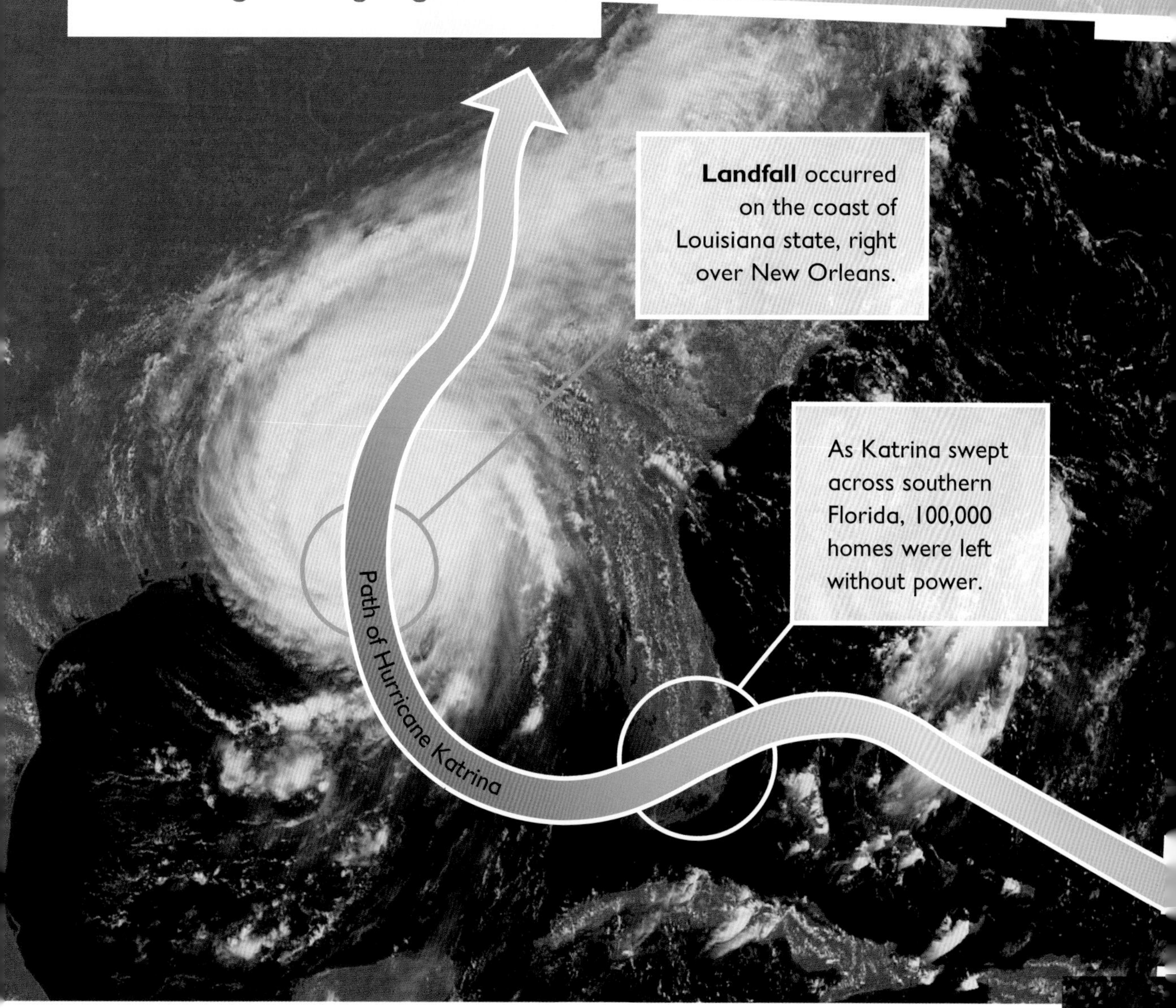

Landfall occurred
on the coast of
Louisiana state, right
over New Orleans.

As Katrina swept
across southern
Florida, 100,000
homes were left
without power.

Path of Hurricane Katrina

landfall when the centre of a hurricane crosses onto land

Watch out, storm about!

Storm spotters can be lifesavers. By warning that a storm is coming, they can give people precious time to prepare for the worst – or at least run for cover.

Weather forecasters collect information from **radar**, weather stations and satellites. Weather satellites keep an eye on the Earth's atmosphere from high above in space. They send back photos and reports about storms. Scientists can then work out how bad storms may get and where they'll go.

Boards protect the glass.

People in Texas, USA, board up their windows after a hurricane warning.

Hurricane hunters

A group of **US** military planes fly right into hurricanes on purpose. They take measurements and send them back to weather forecasters. So far, they've had no crashes.

radar using radio waves to detect and track distant objects

Weather forecasters in Miami, USA, track Hurricane Frances in 2004. The storm caused 49 deaths – but many people were saved by early warnings.

TV crew filming a report from the weather centre.

Weather forecasters discuss the **data**.

FLORIDA

Hurricane Frances

BAHAMAS

Satellite image of the hurricane is displayed on screen.

data information such as numbers, words, pictures and sounds

Seeking supercells

Storm chasers use forecasts, storm warnings and computer data to seek out signs of super-bad weather. When they spot something *really* nasty, they hope it will only get worse.

Supercells are monster thunderstorms. They form when a strong updraft of warm air twists around cold air **currents**. The effects are spectacular and easy to spot.

Balloon carries scientific instruments that measure temperature and other details.

A weather balloon is sent into the heart of a giant supercell.

Super rains

Supercells can bring really heavy rains. In 2005, the Indian city of Mumbai received almost 1 metre (3 feet) of rain in a single day. Most fell in just four hours.

Storm chasers seek out supercells for two main reasons. Firstly, they often last longer than other thunderstorms – between two and six hours. Secondly, a supercell may turn into a storm chaser's number one prize – a tornado.

Storm chasers watch in awe as a mighty supercell forms in Kansas, USA.

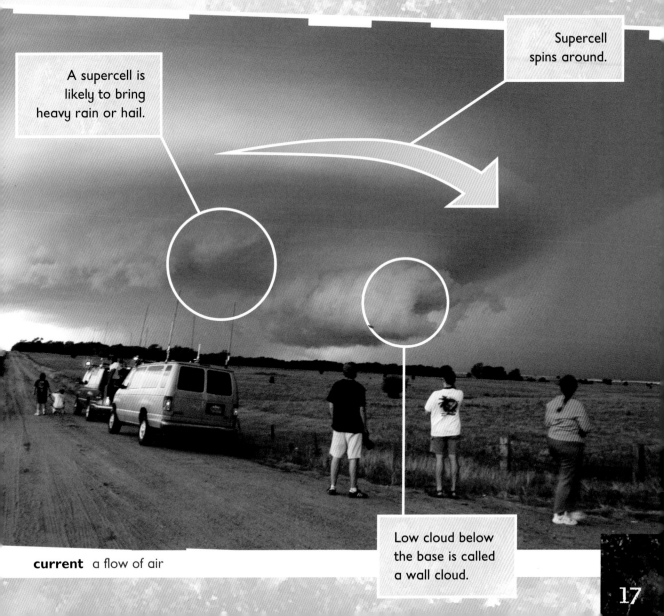

Supercell spins around.

A supercell is likely to bring heavy rain or hail.

Low cloud below the base is called a wall cloud.

current a flow of air

Car chase!

If you're chasing a storm, you need a fast car. You also need some good gadgets. The latest chase vehicles are packed with "mods" for stalking and surviving storms.

Tough TIV

The Tornado Intercept Vehicle (TIV) was once a normal pick-up truck. It's now an armoured beast that can take amazing films of storms. It is built to survive in tornadoes whirling at up to 320 kilometres per hour (199 miles per hour).

A Doppler on Wheels stops at a safe distance to measure the speeds of an Oklahoma thunderstorm.

core the centre of a storm

A Doppler on Wheels does its work from a distance. It sends out radio signals that bounce off a storm and return. These tell the chaser how fast the storm is going and where. Other vehicles, like the TIV, head boldly right into the storm's **core**.

This TIV was specially designed for storm chaser Sean Casey to film right inside a tornado.

A camera in this rotating turret can film in all directions.

Windscreen made of shatterproof plastic, 3.5 cm (1.4 in) thick.

Thick, heavy steel-armour plating

SIDE PANELS DROP DOWN

The vehicle weighs over 6,000 kg (5.9 tons) but can still race around at over 140 km/h (87 mph).

With side panels down, winds can't flip the TIV.

19

Facing danger

Storm chasers are like detectives, trying to work out where and when a storm will strike. But once they're on the chase, it's a risky business — no one can be sure exactly what will happen next.

Storm chasers leave behind **probes** to record the speed, temperature and other data inside a tornado.

The tornado travels at an average speed of 48–64 km/h (30–40 mph).

Debris flies around in the tornado's powerful winds.

probe a device used to test something

Storm chasers beware. Massive forces in storm winds can flip over a car in a second.

Twisting on

Most tornadoes are weak or over very quickly. But the 1925 Tri-State Tornado was different. It lasted for 3.5 hours, travelled through three US states and destroyed 15,000 homes.

Storms can change direction suddenly, flare up violently or die down. This is especially true of tornadoes, which may last for only a few minutes or even seconds. Storm chasers have to work quickly and make fast decisions. If they take a wrong turning in their chase vehicle, they could miss a prize storm!

debris pieces of things that have been destroyed

Fright'ning lightning

Fried alive

US Park Ranger Roy Sullivan was lucky or unlucky, depending on your point of view. He survived being struck by lightning **SEVEN** times between 1942 and 1977!

Water and ice rubbing up against each other... doesn't sound much, does it? But this friction creates the awesome force of lightning, which sizzles the air – beware.

Most lightning zaps between clouds, but it can reach the ground too. That's when it's deadly, striking people directly or setting forests or buildings ablaze. Lightning kills around 1,000 people a year – one in five of those it strikes.

This massive bush fire in California, USA, was caused by lightning. The fire destroyed 67 homes.

friction a force between two things rubbing together

Sizzling air expands...

...creating THUNDER

BANG!

Lightning flashes through the air at up to 50,000 km (31,000 miles) per second!

Punching the core

Some storm chasers are fearless. They take enormous risks to head right into the heart of terrible storms. This is called punching the core.

Before they started to melt, these hailstones were cricket-ball size. Imagine them dropping on your vehicle from way up in the sky!

Core punching is dangerous. The sky goes black. Menacing clouds and rain block out the light, so you can't see more than a stride ahead. In your path there could be a crashed car — or worse, a hidden tornado. That's not all. Many storm cores don't just rain down rain. They hurl down thousands of hailstones — solid balls of ice — enough to make your ears ring with the noise.

Gorilla hail

Giant hailstones are known as gorilla hail. The largest ever in the **USA** fell in 2003 on Aurora, Nebraska. It was as big as a melon!

Digital video camera films storm footage.

Gadgets include **GPS** and radio scanners.

Laptop computer is packed with the latest storm data.

Storm chaser Darren Addy punches the core of a supercell thunderstorm in Kansas, USA.

GPS a system for finding a location using space satellites

Wrecked again

The storm's gone but what's left behind? Devastation, death and chaos – that's what.

Has anyone seen my roof?

Just outside the tornado's path, buildings stand untouched.

The tornado left a 19-km (12-mile) trail of destruction.

In 2008, a tornado ripped through the town of Hautmont, France.

Major storms can flatten towns, leaving thousands of people homeless. As if that's not enough, the heavy rains and damage to **dams** can cause floods that last for days. Fierce storms bring down power lines and rip apart chemical and gas pipes. This can lead to deadly fires and explosions.

Unlucky date

The town of Codell, Kansas, in the USA was damaged by a tornado on 20 May 1916... and again on 20 May 1917... and, would you believe it, by a third tornado on 20 May 1918!

A rescue helicopter hovers over floods in New Orleans, USA, after Hurricane Katrina in 2005.

Three aircraft lie flipped over after a storm had struck central Florida, USA.

dam a barrier built across a river to control the flow of water

Stormy rides

Some people find storms so exciting, they're willing to pay for a front-row seat. You need an experienced guide to get close to a tornado – it could be your money or your life!

Hundreds of storm fans are signing up for organized "storm tours", especially in Tornado Alley. Tour vehicles with storm-chasing experts on board cover hundreds of kilometres every day.

Some reckless **amateurs** chase storms without experience or equipment. They risk their own lives and the lives of others by driving dangerously and ignoring safety warnings. Serious storm chasers call them "yahoos".

Tour director sets up his camera on a **tripod**.

amateur someone who is not professionally trained

Flying high

Storms do the strangest things. In 2006, 19-year-old Matt Suter was picked up by a tornado and flew 400 metres (11,300 feet) before being dumped on the ground. Remarkably, he survived.

Ch-ch-cheese!

Tourists look out — this storm surge could suddenly sweep you out to sea!

A tour group rushes to film a tornado forming outside the town of Happy, Texas, in the USA.

Group weather forecaster runs to grab his instruments.

Two tourists nervously film the approaching storm.

tripod a three-legged stand for keeping a camera steady

29

Glossary

amateur someone who is not professionally trained

atmosphere the layer of gases that surround the Earth

core the centre of a storm

current a flow of air

dam a barrier built across a river to control the flow of water

data information such as numbers, words, pictures and sounds

debris pieces of things that have been destroyed

friction a force between two things rubbing together

GPS (Global Positioning System) a system for finding a location using space satellites

landfall when the centre of a hurricane crosses onto land

probe a device used to test something

radar using radio waves to detect and track distant objects

satellite a machine that is sent into space to collect and send back information

storm surge a swell of water pushed to the shore by storm winds

swarm a series of tornadoes produced by the same storm

tornado a spinning, funnel-shaped windstorm

tripod a three-legged stand for keeping a camera steady

updraft a flow of air upwards

vacuum a completely empty, airless space

vortex a whirling mass of air that sucks in everything near it

Further information

Books

Turbulent Planet: Storm Warning by Chris Oxlade (Raintree, 2005)
A great guide to tornadoes and other types of storm.

Adventures in Tornado Alley: The Storm Chasers by Mike Hollingshead, Eric Nguyen and Chuck Doswell (Thames & Hudson, 2008)
Stunning photographs of storms by leading storm chasers.

Eye of the Storm by Jeffery Rosenfeld (Basic Books, 2003)
This book takes readers inside the world's deadly tornadoes and hurricanes as well as snow blizzards.

Hurricane Hunters and Tornado Chasers by Gary Jeffery (Rosen Publishing Group, 2008)
An exciting new book about storm chasing.

Websites

www.ukstorm.net
An amateur storm chaser's site with lots of photos and videos of storms in the UK and the USA.

www.stormchaser.com
Thrill at the pictures, videos and stories from the website of Warren Faidley, one of the world's most experienced storm chasers.

www.spc.noaa.gov
The Storm Prediction Centre has amazing real-time images of storms brewing over the USA.

www.skydiary.com/kids
An excellent website giving lots of information on storm types and what it is like to chase a storm.

www.nssl.noaa.gov/faq/faq_tor.php
Tornadoes, thunderstorms and lightning are explained in detail at the National Severe Storms Laboratory website.

Films

Twister directed by Jan de Bont (Warner Brothers, 1996)
Real storm chasers scoffed at some of the technical mistakes, but you'll love the special effects in this movie about tornadoes.

Storm Chasers (Discovery Channel, 2007)
This TV series follows senior storm chasers Dr Josh Wurman and Sean Casey as they hunt down serious storms.

Tornado Glory directed by Ken Cole (Ken Cole Productions, 2004)
An amazing documentary about storms and storm chasers. You can learn more and see footage at **www.tornadoglory.com.**

Index